CONTROLLING MOISTURE IN HOMES

National Association of Home Builders
15th and M Streets, N.W.
Washington, D.C. 20005

Controlling Moisture in Homes
ISBN 0-86718-302-0
Library of Congress Catalog Card Number 87-62883
Copyright © 1987 by the
National Association of Home Builders of the United States
15th and M Streets, N.W.
Washington, D.C. 20005

All rights reserved. No part of this book may be reproduced or utilized in any form or by any means, electronic or mechanical, including photocopying and recording, or by an information storage and retrieval system without permission in writing from the publisher. When ordering this publication, please provide the following information:

Title
ISBN 0-86718-302-0
Price
Quantity
NAHB membership number (as it appears on *Builder* or *Nation's Business News* label)
Mailing address (including street number and zip code)

Contents

Introduction 5

Chapter 1. Moisture Migration 7
   Condensation 7
   Diffusion 9
   Air Flow 10

Chapter 2. Types of Moisture Problems 13
   Interior Surfaces 13
   Exterior Surfaces 13
   Swelling and Buckling 14
   Decay 14
   Insulation 14

Chapter 3. Moisture Control in Cold Climates 15
   Indoor Humidity 15
   Walls 17
   Attics and Roof Spaces 20
   Crawl Spaces 23
   Concrete Slab Floors 25
   Basements 25
   Good Practice Recommendations 25

Chapter 4. Moisture Control in Warm, Humid Climates 29
   Indoor Humidity 29
   Vapor Retarders 30
   Masonry Walls 30
   Good Practice Recommendations 31

Chapter 5. Correcting Existing Problems 33
   High Relative Humidity 33
   Window Condensation 34
   Attic Moisture 34
   Crawl Space Moisture 35
   Concrete Surface Condensation 35
   Exterior Paint Peeling 35
   Ice Dams 36

References 37

Appendix: Psychrometrics for Builders and Designers:
The Behavior of Moist Air 41

Acknowledgments

Controlling Moisture in Homes was prepared by the NAHB National Research Center for the National Association of Home Builders through the NAHB Standing Committee on Research. The project was directed by Donald F. Luebs, Director of Building Systems, NAHB/NRC, with contributions from Gerald E. Sherwood, P.E., formerly with the USDA Forest Products Laboratory, Madison, WI; Ralph J. Johnson, President Emeritus, NAHB/NRC; Bion D. Howard, NAHB Technical Services Department; and Heinz R. Trechsel, consultant to the building industry.

This publication was produced by the National Association of Home Builders under the direction of Kent Colton, NAHB Executive Vice President, in association with NAHB staff members James E. Johnson, Jr., Staff Vice President, Information Services; Denise L. Darling, Staff Vice President, Publishing Services; Susan D. Bradford, Publications Director; Curt Hane, Editor; and David Rhodes, Art Director.

Introduction

Moisture control is a major concern of the home building industry. Moisture problems can range from simple nuisances to serious conditions that threaten the structural integrity of a building. High humidities may result in condensation on windows and the formation of mildew on interior surfaces. Moisture can cause warping and paint failure in wood siding products and corrosion of metal fasteners and hardware. Excessive, long-term moisture can produce decay in a wood structure.

Moisture in vapor form (humidity) is not usually a problem. However, it may become a problem when vapor condenses as free water on cold surfaces. This book examines both the mechanisms of moisture movement and condensation, and methods for controlling this movement to prevent or correct problems in new and existing homes.

Condensation problems in houses were of little consequence prior to the introduction of thermal insulation and tighter construction. In an effort to control the indoor environment more closely, builders began using thermal insulation during the 1930s. However, condensation problems occasionally appeared in walls and attics in which the insulation resulted in lowering the temperature of wall or roof sheathing surfaces below the temperature at which water vapor condenses, or the dew point temperature.

At a national meeting soon thereafter, a group of scientists involved in building research suggested that a barrier was needed to prevent moisture vapor in the indoor air from moving out to these cold surfaces. From that meeting, the term *vapor barrier* and the concept of its use were developed, and a test was devised to measure the rate of water vapor movement through a material. The perm (the term designated for measuring this permeability) rating was calculated in such a way that one perm or less indicated that the material was considered to be a vapor barrier. Since perm is a rate of moisture flow, the lower the perm rating, the better the vapor barrier.

A common misconception holds that vapor barriers stop all moisture movement. In truth, they only slow that movement. To discourage this misconception, the American Society of Heating, Refrigerating and Air-Conditioning Engineers (ASHRAE) and the American Society for Testing and Materials (ASTM) recently adopted the term *vapor retarder*, the term used throughout this book.

Vapor retarders adequately controlled condensation for many years. When the energy crisis of the 1970s resulted in even higher levels of insulation and more effective methods to reduce outdoor air infiltration, the potential for condensation increased in two ways:

- The added insulation resulted in colder inside sheathing surfaces.
- Tighter houses meant higher indoor relative humidities because less indoor moisture was lost through exchange with the outdoor air, which usually contains much less moisture in cold weather.

Under these conditions, more moisture finds its way into walls and attics by diffusion through ineffective vapor retarders or through air leaks and results in destructive condensation. Therefore, more attention needs to be given to installing vapor retarders effectively and to reducing humidity in the house. While much attention is usually focused on cold weather condensation, problems can also exist where air conditioning is used for extended periods in warm, humid climates.

The science of moisture movement and control is not an exact one. Data for the many variables involved are difficult to establish. While research to quantify these variables is continuing, much is known about building practices that have proven effective. This study presents current, prevailing information on moisture control from the scientific and building communities that should prove valuable to home builders throughout the country.

Chapter 1
Moisture Migration

Moisture migrates from a point of high concentration to a point of lower concentration by two methods:
- diffusion through materials
- air flow carrying moisture with it

Most moisture movement theories have been established around diffusion, but more recent observations suggest that air flow can also be a major factor in moisture transport in conventional building construction. Regardless of how the moisture is transported, the dew point of the air—relative to the temperature of surfaces with which the air comes into contact—is critical to the formation of condensation.

Condensation

The amount of moisture vapor in the atmosphere is expressed as a percentage of the total amount that the air can hold at a given temperature. Warm air can hold more moisture in the vapor phase than cold air. Therefore, when air containing a given amount of moisture vapor is cooled, the relative humidity will increase and eventually reach 100 percent, at which point the excess moisture will begin to condense out. The temperature that causes the water vapor to condense to a liquid is the dew point. Moisture condenses out of the air onto surfaces that are below the dew point temperature, which explains why moisture condenses on a glass of ice water when the glass surface is below the dew point temperature of the air.

Condensation can also occur within structural cavities such as walls and attics. The two critical factors for condensation are relative humidity of the air and the temperature of surfaces. Figure 1 shows a psychrometric chart that can be used to determine the dew point temperature for a surface under different temperature and relative humidity conditions. For example, if the air in a wall cavity has a temperature of 60°F and a relative humidity of 70 percent, condensation will occur on the inner side of wall sheathing if that inner wall is below 50°F, the temperature at which the relative humidity becomes 100 percent. The appendix on page 41 describes other practical applications of this chart in solving moisture-related problems.

When condensation occurs, the liquid moisture may be absorbed by the material providing the condensing surface or may move through the material in liquid form. Ultimately, it may drain away or evaporate back into the vapor phase when the air temperature increases. A

Figure 1: Simplified psychrometric chart showing determination of dew point temperature of air at 60°F, 70 percent relative humidity.

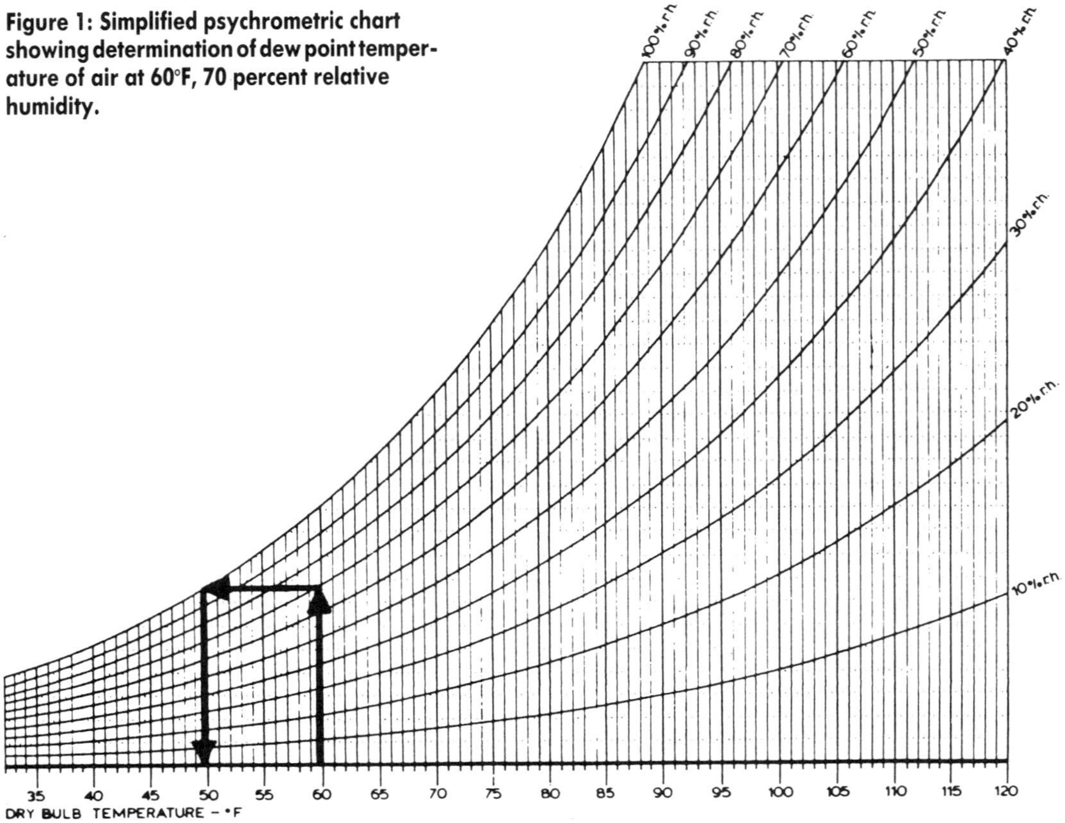

condensing surface below freezing temperature tends to accentuate the problem because the moisture may accumulate as frost or ice, which can build up until warmer weather melts it all at once. However, frost and ice are not always a problem, since they may transpire directly back to the vapor phase without melting, a process called sublimation. Also, daily and seasonal temperature swings will often minimize or eliminate problems by allowing the liquid moisture to evaporate before it causes any damage.

Diffusion

Water vapor is a gas. As such, it can diffuse or pass directly through building materials without wetting them. Diffusion of water vapor through a material depends on the difference in vapor pressure (a function of relative humidity) between the two sides of the material and on the permeability of the material. Table 1 shows perm ratings of some typical building materials.

Table 1: Perm Rating for Selected Building Materials
(ASTM E-96 dry cup method)

Material	Thickness/Weight	Perm Rating*
Gypsum wall board	.375 in.	50
Structural insulating board	.5 in.	50-90
Hardboard (standard)	.125 in.	11
Plywood (exterior glue)	.25 in.	0.7
Saturated and coated roll roofing	65 lb.	0.05
Asphalt coated paper (insulation backing)	6.2 lb.	0.4
Asphalt felt (building paper)	15 lb.	1.0
Aluminum foil	0.00035 in.	0.05
Polyethylene	6 mil.	0.06
Polyethylene	4 mil.	0.08
Expanded polystyrene (extruded)	1 in.	1.2
Expanded polystyrene (bead)	1 in.	2.0-5.8
Vapor retarder paint	0.0031 in.	0.45

*Materials with a perm rating of 1.0 or less are considered to be vapor retarders.

Source: American Society of Heating, Refrigerating and Air-Conditioning Engineers. *ASHRAE Handbook of Fundamentals.* New York: ASHRAE, 1985.

While any material with a perm rating less than one is generally considered to be a vapor retarder, materials with much lower ratings are now normally used in new construction. Vapor-retarding paints may be helpful in retrofit work if no other method is feasible, but their use without an actual vapor retarder is not usually considered adequate in new construction.

The most common design or analysis method for diffusion is called the moisture profile method or the dew point method, described in the *ASHRAE Handbook of Fundamentals*. If diffusion were the only means of transport, this method would establish—with a good degree of accuracy—where condensation will occur. However, air flow containing moisture vapor usually complicates actual moisture movement.

Air Flow

Air flow can carry moist indoor air into wall cavities and attic spaces, permitting moisture vapor to condense on cold surfaces. Air flow depends not on vapor pressure differences (as does diffusion), but on indoor-outdoor air pressure differences. The amount of moisture carried depends on the rate of air flow and the moisture content of the air. Air passes through cracks and openings in walls and ceilings created by joints between the wall and floor, penetrations of electrical outlets and light fixtures, cracks around windows and doors, and loose-fitting attic access doors.

Indoor air pressure that is higher than outdoor pressure is usually caused by either wind or stack effect. Wind pressures cause both infiltration and exfiltration. Pressure differentials across the walls and roof depend on such factors as wind speed, wind direction, terrain, landscaping and shape of the building. The main moisture transport from wind is through the walls opposite the windward side (Figure 2). Stack effect is a result of the difference between indoor and outdoor temperatures. The warm, lighter indoor air tends to rise and move out through cracks and openings in the ceiling and upper parts of the wall. This movement reduces the pressure in the lower part of the house, resulting in cold outside air entering through the floor or lower walls (Figure 3). This effect is greater in two-story houses than in one-story houses because of the additional height.

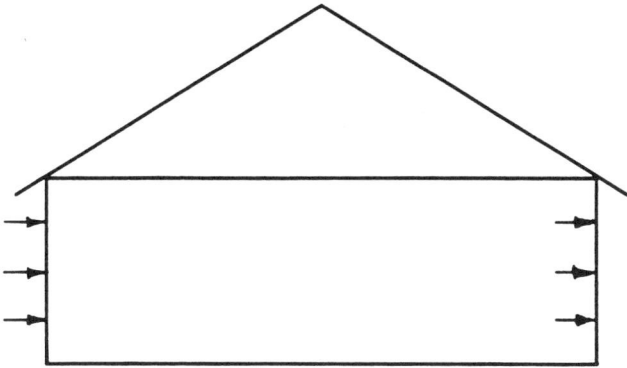

Figure 2: Wind creates pressure differences that cause air to flow out through the wall opposite the windward side. Some air may also flow out through the ceiling, depending on the shape of the house and location of attic vents.

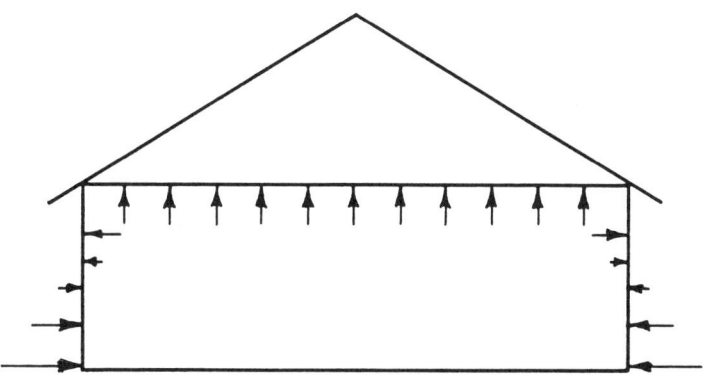

Figure 3: The stack effect of warm air rising causes air to move out through cracks and openings in the upper part of the house while drawing in outside air through cracks and openings in the lower part of the house.

Chapter 2
Types of Moisture Problems

A certain amount of condensation occurs occasionally in almost all houses. In most cases, the condensation does not cause a problem. Some materials are able to absorb and store this moisture for short periods and return it to the air when conditions change. When condensation occurs on the bottom of roof sheathing during the night, the moisture is usually driven back into the air when the sun shines on the roof during the day or when the air temperature rises. This type of daily cycling may also occur in walls. Condensation may occur in walls for a period of several days during times of extreme cold. If it evaporates at the end of that time, no damage will result.

The existence of a problem depends on such factors as the quantity of condensation, its duration, the absorbency of the building materials, the temperature, and the ability of the excess moisture to eventually escape. Adverse effects of a moisture problem may include mildew or paint failure on finished surfaces, swelling or buckling of wood-based materials, corrosion of metal fasteners or hardware, reduced effectiveness of some insulation materials, and, in extreme cases over prolonged periods, decay of the wood structure.

Interior Surfaces

High relative humidity can result in stain or mildew on interior finish surfaces. For mildew growth, the surface must be near dew point temperature. Surface temperatures below dew point will result in condensation. Such temperatures sometimes exist at exterior wall corners or at wall/ceiling joints, areas that are often underinsulated.

Mildew or condensation may also develop over drywall nail heads because the high thermal conductivity of the nail results in a colder surface. Occasionally, such problems also arise over exterior wall studs or ceiling joists because the thermal conductivity of these members is greater than the wall or ceiling insulation. Window sash and trim may also become stained by excessive condensation running off the glass.

Exterior Surfaces

Paint peeling, staining, and streaking on exterior siding and trim can result from condensation. Moisture moving out through cold walls may condense on the back of cold siding. Staining or streaking may result when the condensed moisture runs out from between the courses of siding, carrying dirt and water-soluble extractives from the wood with it. In other cases, water may migrate through the siding and stain the surface or accumulate behind the exterior paint, causing blistering.

Exterior sources of moisture, primarily rain, can cause similar problems if the siding is not properly installed and finished, so care should be taken to identify the source of the problem correctly.

Swelling and Buckling

Wood products swell as their moisture content increases. Doors and windows may stick, and wall and roof sheathing, siding, and interior paneling may buckle between fasteners and supports. These materials are normally dry as manufactured; thus, increases in moisture may cause significant expansion. Although the most noticeable effect is aesthetic, buckling may loosen nails, open joints, cause splits, or produce other conditions that lead to structural deterioration.

Decay

Wetting of wood or wood products by condensation over a long period of time can create conditions for decay. Serious problems can occur in roof soffits, sheathing, and framing; in subfloors and floor framing; and in wall siding, sheathing, and framing. Decay can also occur in window sash and trim and around doors, particularly at the sill.

Growth of decay fungi requires moisture, oxygen, and a temperature of 40°F or higher. In many cases, decay does not become a problem because condensation occurs on cold surfaces during the winter when temperatures are too low to support the growth of decay fungi, and warm weather causes the moisture to dissipate before decay begins to occur.

Insulation

In severe cases, trapped moisture in insulation can reduce the R-value and produce other undesirable results, particularly in absorbent organic materials such as cellulose. Condensation is unlikely to occur within permeable insulation in a wall cavity. However, condensation can occur at the interface of the insulation and the wall sheathing. Unless the material is especially absorbent, only a thin layer of insulation near the sheathing is usually affected.

In ceilings, condensation can be a greater problem because gravity moves moisture down through the insulation. This moisture reduces the insulation's R-value and can eventually stain the ceiling. However, studies at the U. S. Forest Products Laboratory have shown that excess moisture vapor in a properly ventilated attic space will usually dissipate harmlessly into the air before condensing.

Chapter 3
Moisture Control in Cold Climates

Most moisture problems in homes are associated with cold weather. Indoor relative humidity is the controlling factor. This concern and others are addressed in this chapter as they apply to walls, attics, crawl spaces, and basements under cold weather conditions.

Under cold weather conditions, moisture is usually controlled by a combination of measures:

- regulation of indoor humidity
- use of vapor retarders
- reduction of air leakage from conditioned spaces
- ventilation of attic and crawl spaces

Indoor Humidity

The first step in preventing moisture damage is to maintain a reasonable indoor relative humidity of between 30 and 40 percent during the heating season. When indoor humidity exceeds 50 percent during cold weather, adverse effects begin to appear. A lower indoor relative humidity will always reduce the potential for condensation, but keep in mind that exceptionally dry conditions can result in respiratory irritation and shrinking of wood furniture and trim.

It is virtually impossible, even with properly installed vapor retarders, to construct a house that will not harbor some condensation when the indoor humidity exceeds 40 or 50 percent. When a house is retrofitted with insulation without the benefit of vapor retarders and air leakage control, a much lower humidity may be required. Persistent condensation on double-glazed windows is a good indicator that relative humidity is too high and may be causing hidden moisture accumulations in other parts of the structure.

Prior to the mid-1970s, humidity control was generally limited to instructing homeowners using humidifiers to set them at a maximum of 35 percent relative humidity and to lower the setting when the outdoor temperature fell below 20°F. In recent years, efforts to tighten up houses have essentially eliminated the need for mechanical humidification. Unfortunately, these same efforts have occasionally resulted in undesirably high levels of indoor humidity. With infiltration levels reduced to 0.4 air changes per hour or less in many cases, moisture from cooking, bathing, respiration, and house plants can sometimes cause indoor humidity to exceed 40 percent, especially in smaller homes.

Exhaust vents can provide some humidity control in kitchens and bathrooms. These may be manually controlled by a conscientious homeowner or automatically controlled by humidistats that activate the fan when the relative humidity exceeds a predetermined level.

In houses with forced-air heating systems, a more effective method involves connecting a small duct leading from the outdoors to the return side of the duct system. With this method, fresh air is drawn into the house each time the system operates. A damper in the fresh air duct will allow the occupant to adjust the level of incoming air. While such ventilation results in additional energy requirements to heat the incoming air, a house incorporating this system is more energy efficient than a leaky house with uncontrolled natural air exchange. By properly adjusting fresh air ventilation to the individual needs of a household, the benefits of energy-efficient construction are preserved.

An alternative to direct ventilation is the use of an air-to-air heat exchanger. This equipment can recover 50 percent or more of the heat from air being exhausted to the outdoors and exchange it to the incoming air (Figure 4). However, the initial cost—along with operation and maintenance costs—should be carefully considered in relation to the value of the energy savings that this method can produce compared to direct ventilation without heat recovery. Also, it should be noted that air-to-air heat exchangers can be a significant source of air leakage when not in operation.

Portable dehumidifiers are sometimes used to reduce indoor humidity. However, in cases of excessive humidity in cold weather, portable

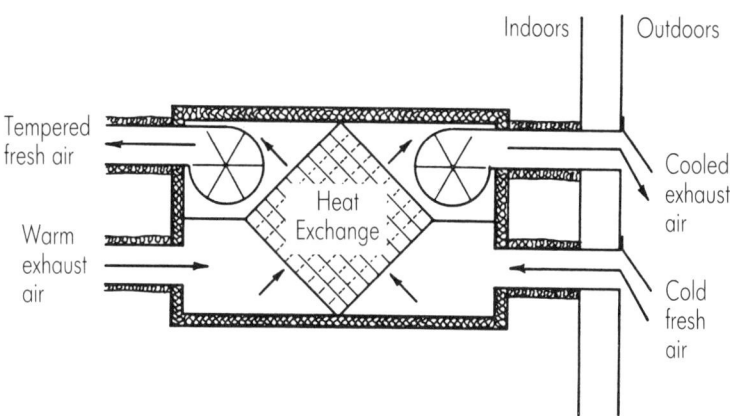

Figure 4: Air-to-air heat exchanger illustrating the transfer of heat from outgoing exhaust air to incoming fresh air.

dehumidifiers are usually not adequate. The most effective measure is usually to search out and control the moisture sources rather than to depend on a dehumidifier to solve an existing problem.

Excess moisture vapor can also escape through the ceiling if a ceiling vapor retarder is not present. Experience has shown that omitting ceiling vapor retarders can be considered in areas where the design temperature is above −20°F. This measure applies only under those circumstances in which a properly ventilated attic space is provided. (See section on attics and roof spaces.)

Special moisture-control measures are essential in rooms containing a hot tub, spa, or swimming pool. Such rooms should be separated from the rest of the house with airtight doors. A separate heating system should also be provided, with good mechanical ventilation to the outdoors. Pay particularly close attention to vapor retarder installation in both walls and ceilings of these rooms. Avoid the use of recessed lights in the ceiling; they puncture the vapor retarder. In cold climates, it may be necessary to use triple glazing or special low conductance windows to prevent window condensation in a pool or spa room. Finally, the pool or spa should be tightly covered to minimize evaporation when not in use.

Walls

Moisture control in walls has traditionally focused on the use of vapor retarders on the warm-in-winter side of the wall. The asphalted paper backing on some blanket insulation is technically a vapor retarder and will generally provide adequate protection, particularly if the paper flanges are installed to overlap each other over the studs. For the most effective protection, however, wide sheets of polyethylene should cover an entire wall, extending behind partition intersections, with accurate cutouts provided for windows, doors, and electrical boxes (Figure 5). This method ensures continuous coverage of all surface areas, including framing. While 2-mil polyethylene provides adequate vapor resistance, 4-mil polyethylene is preferred because of its increased resistance to tearing during installation.

While the diffusion of water vapor through the materials of the wall has long been recognized as a dominant means of moisture transfer, air leakage into the wall cavity may be equally important when a vapor retarder is otherwise used. Moisture-laden air can enter the wall through joints and cracks at the base of the wall, around windows and doors, or through electrical switches and outlets. All such openings and penetrations should be made as airtight as possible to eliminate leakage. Vapor retarder materials such as polyethylene can serve as air barriers, but only if they are continuous. To be effective, the materials

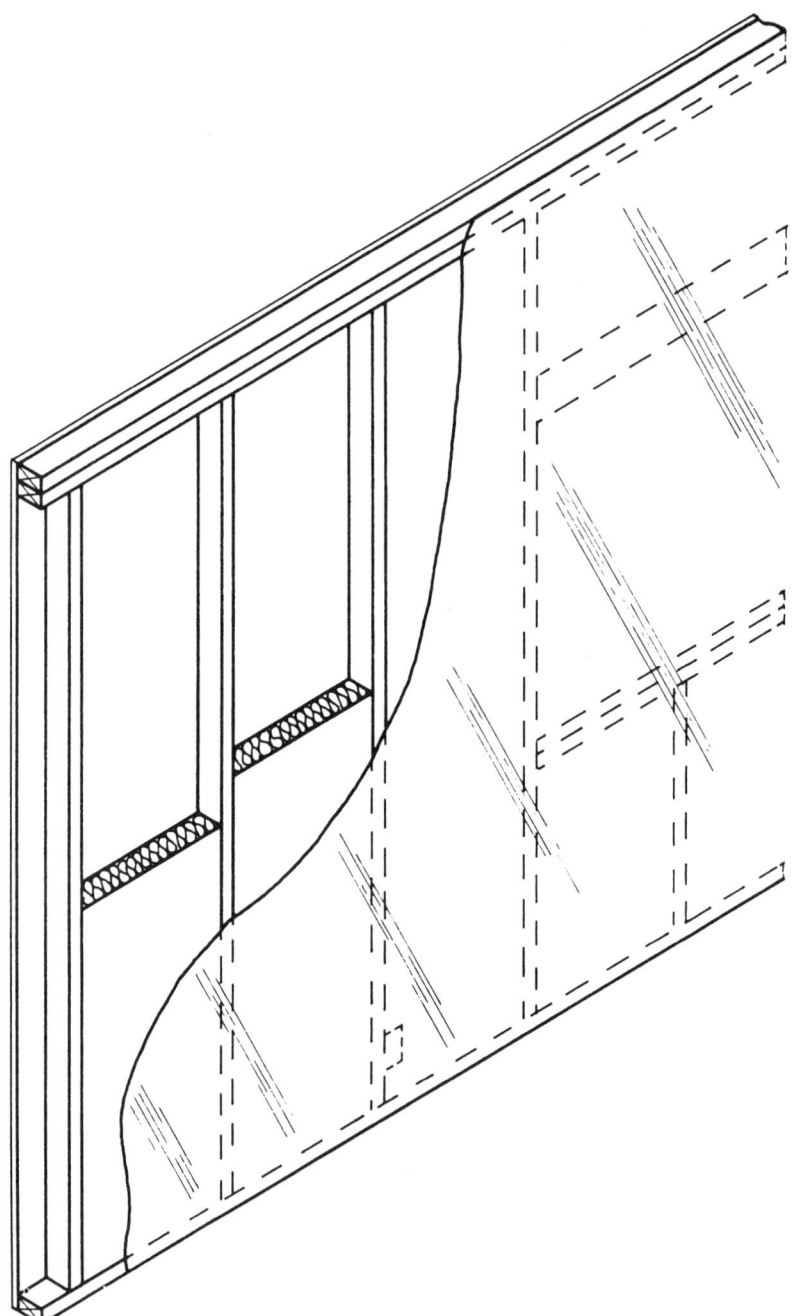

Figure 5: Large sheets of polyethylene vapor retarder provide continuous coverage over the entire wall surface. The vapor retarder should be carefully cut to fit tightly at openings and should be taped securely at electrical boxes and similar penetrations.

must be accurately fitted around window and door openings and be taped securely around electrical boxes. Resilient gaskets may be used behind the cover plates of outlets and switches for additional protection.

The need for vapor retarders depends on geographic location. With the United States divided into three climatic zones (Figure 6), vapor retarders are recommended on the warm-in-winter face of insulated walls in Zones 1 and 2, including Alaska. Vapor retarders are not required in the mild climate of Hawaii. Application of vapor retarders in Zone 3 is discussed in a later section.

In the past, most experts advocated high permeability for materials on the outside of the wall to allow any moisture in the wall to escape to the outside. While this practice is still advisable with traditional wall sheathing products, some plastic foam sheathings present a different condition. Materials such as extruded polystyrene and foil-faced foam boards act as both vapor retarders and insulators. Therefore, the inside face of the sheathing will typically remain above dew point temperature. Obviously, in very cold climates, greater thicknesses of plastic foam sheathing will be required to keep the temperature of the inside face above the dew point.

Some sources have previously suggested ventilating wall cavities to allow moisture to escape, particularly where low permeability sheathing, such as insulating foam, is used. However, studies by the U.S. Forest Products Laboratory have shown that ventilating can actually

Figure 6: Climatic zones defined by winter design temperatures. Adapted from the *ASHRAE Handbook of Fundamentals*.

increase the potential for condensation problems. Vents provided only at the top tend to draw humid indoor air into the wall cavity, increasing the potential for moisture condensation. Vents provided at both top and bottom allow cold air to pass through the wall, which may reduce the effectiveness of insulation and cool the sheathing surface below dew point temperature. In either case, the unwanted result may be increased condensation.

Attics and Roof Spaces

The principal moisture-control measure for attics and roof spaces is ventilation. Ceiling vapor retarders reduce the rate of moisture movement through the ceiling, which, in turn, reduces ventilation requirements. As with walls, the most effective ceiling vapor retarder is wide sheets of 4-mil polyethylene. For maximum effectiveness, the vapor retarder should extend over the top plate of interior partitions and be sealed around all penetrations, such as lighting fixtures and vent stacks. Also, attic access doors should be insulated and tightly sealed with weatherstripping. Ceiling vapor retarders are recommended for all roofs in Zone 1 and for cathedral ceilings and flat roofs in Zones 1 and 2.

Ventilation recommendations are stated as a ratio of vent area to ceiling area with the stipulation that vents be located to provide cross ventilation of the attic or roof space. One square foot of net vent-free area for each 300 square feet of ceiling area is recommended with a ceiling vapor retarder. Without a vapor retarder, the recommended vent area is doubled, except that it need not be doubled if at least one half of the vent area is located in the upper portion of the space (at least three feet above the eave), with the balance provided by eave or soffit vents (Figure 7). Where louvers and screening are used, the gross vent area should be increased (Table 2).

Table 2: Conversion Factors to Obtain Net Free Area from Gross Vent Area.

Type of Covering			Area of Opening
$1/4''$	hardware cloth		same as required for net free area
$1/4''$	hardware cloth and rain louvers	2	times required net free area
$1/8''$	mesh screen	1.25	times required net free area
$1/8''$	mesh screen and rain louvers	2.25	times required net free area
$1/16''$	mesh screen	2	times required net free area
$1/16''$	mesh screen and rain louvers	3	times required net free area

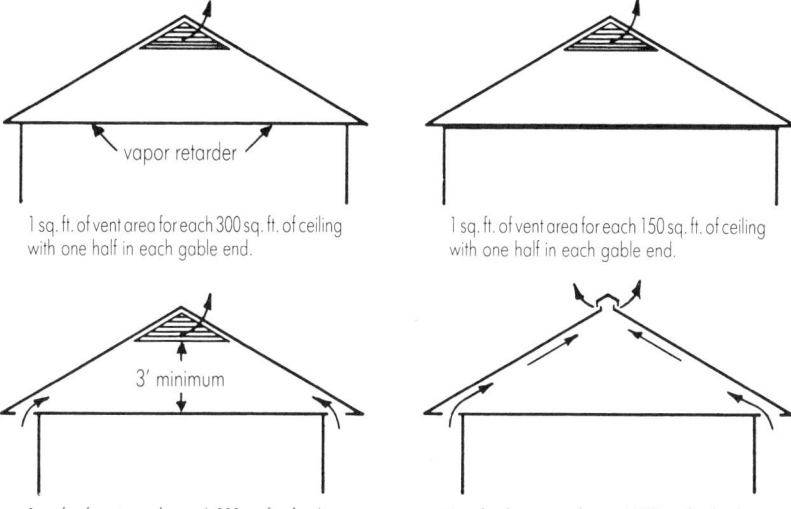

Figure 7: Recommended attic ventilation in net area for different combinations of vents with and without a ceiling vapor retarder.

Current ceiling insulation practice with thicknesses of six inches or more may require special measures to prevent blocking eave vents. One solution utilizes a cantilevered roof truss to provide added height above the outside wall (Figure 8). This construction permits the insulation to extend over the top plate of the wall with a ventilation space between the insulation and the underside of roof sheathing. Another solution calls for the installation of ventilation tunnels between trusses

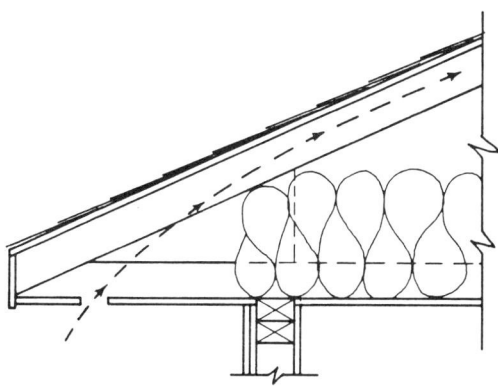

Figure 8: A cantilevered truss construction may be used to provide a passageway for ventilation air from soffit vents where thick insulation would otherwise interfere.

or rafters to provide a passageway for ventilation, particularly when loose fill insulation is used (Figure 9). Good ventilation will help to prevent the formation of ice dams. When poor ventilation results in a warmer attic, snow tends to melt and run down to the roof overhang, where it refreezes. The resulting ice can build up to form a trough that catches water at a point directly over the house wall (Figure 10). The water then backs up under the shingles and runs down through the roof, ceiling, soffit, and/or wall, causing stains on interior drywall, exterior paint peeling, or worse. These symptoms are sometimes mistaken for condensation in the wall or ceiling. Good ceiling insulation and attic ventilation will keep the roof at temperatures near the outdoor air temperature and delay melting until warmer weather when ice dams will not form. In areas where ice dams are prevalent, a strip of roll roofing offers extra protection when installed under the shingles parallel to the eave, extending from the edge of the roof to at least one foot inside of the exterior wall line. This additional precaution ensures that, if an ice dam does occur, water will not get through the roof.

Flat roofs are particularly vulnerable to condensation because they rely primarily on wind pressures for ventilation and are usually vented at the perimeter only. Good vapor retarder protection is critical in flat roofs in Zones 1 and 2. It is important to prevent air leakage at interior partitions and around recessed lighting, vent stacks, and other penetrations in the vapor retarder.

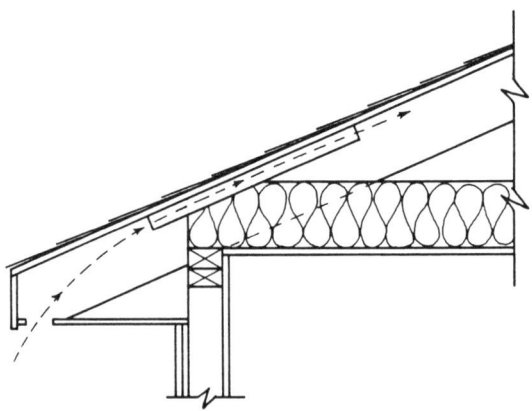

Figure 9. A vent tunnel of fiberboard or other material will provide a passageway for ventilation air from soffit vents where thicker insulation is used with conventional trusses or framing.

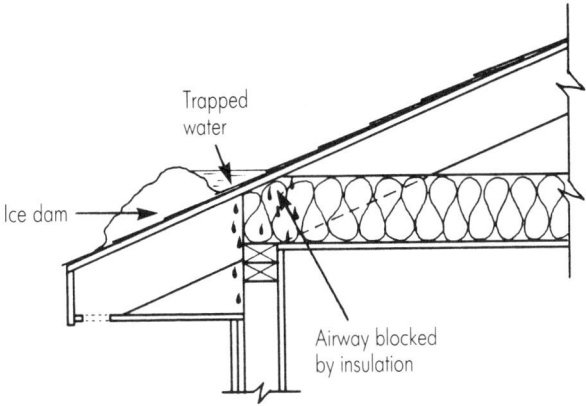

Figure 10: Ice dams may develop when snow on the roof melts in cold weather. Good ceiling insulation and well-distributed ventilation will minimize this problem by avoiding warm spots in the attic.

Cathedral ceilings are particularly vulnerable to condensation. Warm air in the roof cavity rises from both sides of the roof and is blocked at the peak unless it can escape. In conjunction with a good ceiling vapor retarder, a combination of vents at the eaves and the ridge is suggested to avoid this condition in Zones 1 and 2.

Some sources have suggested that, like walls, flat roofs and cathedral ceilings need not be ventilated when an effective vapor retarder is used. While a vapor retarder may be an effective means to control condensation, it may also lead to excessive buildup of heat in the summer and premature failure of the roofing.

Crawl Spaces

The principal source of moisture in crawl spaces is the soil. Moisture from the soil can create excessive humidity that may condense on floor framing members.

In problem-prone areas, a soil cover should always be used. The soil cover should be a heavy, vapor-retarding material that is tear and puncture resistant. The material should be laid on the soil with all joints lapped 8-12 inches and held in place with bricks or other weights (Figure 11). Some builders cover the entire surface with a thin bed of sand or gravel—or even a thin concrete slab—to ensure that it remains in place. While roll roofing was used as a soil cover for many years, 6-mil polyethylene has now become the preferred material.

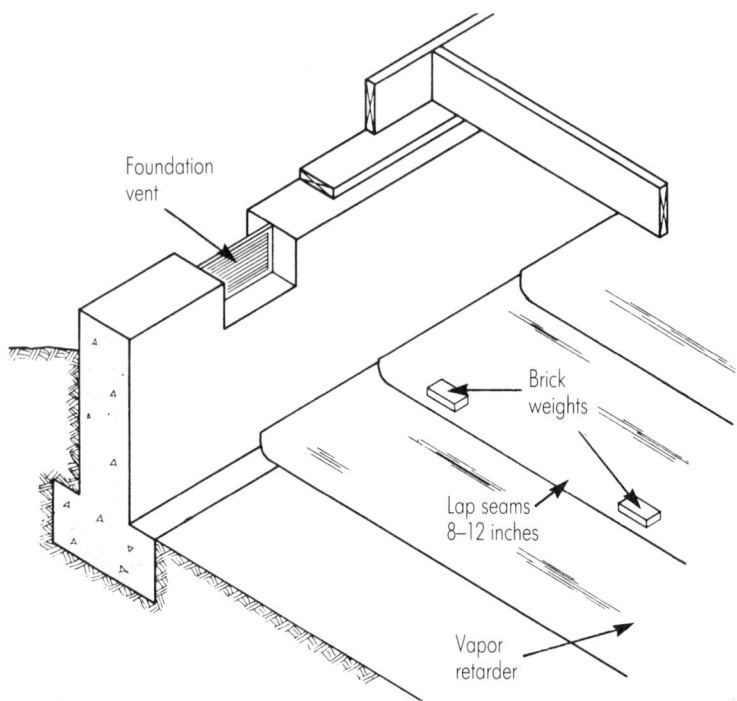

Figure 11: A 6-mil polyethylene vapor retarder laid over the soil is the primary means of controlling moisture in a crawl space. Seams should be lapped 8-12 inches and held in place with bricks or other weights, or the entire surface covered with a thin bed of sand or gravel, or a thin concrete slab.

Ventilation recommendations are stated as a ratio of vent area to soil surface area. With a good soil cover, one square foot of net vent area is generally recommended for each 1500 square feet of soil area. Vents should be located to provide cross ventilation of the crawl space, which normally means a minimum of two openings placed on opposite walls. Drainage away from the foundation can be critical, since water standing on top of the soil cover renders the cover useless. In problem areas, a sump drain or pump may be needed. Where a soil cover is not used, the ventilation should be increased to one square foot for each 150 square feet of soil area with at least four vents, one near each corner of the space.

In insulated floors, the vapor retarder should always be on the warm-in-winter side; thus, in cold climates, it should be up against the subfloor. A vapor retarder on the bottom of the insulation may trap moisture during cold weather. Generally, a bottom-side vapor retarder should never be used in the floor over a crawl space.

Concrete Slab Floors

When a house is built on a concrete slab floor, a moisture-retarding membrane should be placed under the slab to prevent soil moisture from rising into the house. The material should be tear and puncture resistant, such as 6-mil polyethylene. Except in dry, well-drained soils, three to four inches of sand or gravel should be used under the polyethylene film to act as a water capillarity break. To prevent condensation on the slab in cold weather, perimeter insulation should be used around the foundation to keep the slab above the dew point temperature of the indoor air.

Basements

Basement walls present a special problem because moisture can move in either direction. Moisture from the exterior should be stopped with a masonry paint or coating on the outside of the wall above grade, and a waterproof coating and/or a moisture- retarding membrane below grade. A plastic film such as 6-mil polyethylene, lap-sealed with adhesive or tape, is recommended below grade. The top edge of the film should be adhered to the wall to prevent surface water from getting between the wall and the film.

If an insulated finished wall is constructed on the inside, a vapor retarder should be used on the warm-in-winter side (Figure 12). Even though this installation may technically result in a vapor retarder on both sides, it has been shown to be effective. Another alternative is the installation of closed-cell plastic foam insulation on either the interior or exterior of the basement wall. The insulation itself is a vapor retarder; therefore, resistance to water vapor movement is provided in both directions. Technically, the best location for the foam insulation is the exterior of the wall. If used on the exterior, it must be covered with a weather-resistant material, such as cement board, above grade. If used on the inside, plastic foam insulation must be covered with a fire-resistant material, such as gypsumboard.

Good Practice Recommendations

- Maintain an indoor relative humidity of 30-50 percent during cold weather. Exhaust fans operated either manually or by a humidistat can be effective. Where applicable, a damper-controlled fresh air duct to the return side of a forced air heating system can be particularly effective.
- Install vapor retarders on the warm-in-winter side of walls, on ceilings below flat roofs and on cathedral ceilings in all heating climates (Zones 1 and 2), and on ceilings below attics in cold climates (Zone 1). For continuous coverage and good tear resistance, a 4-mil polyethylene film is suggested.

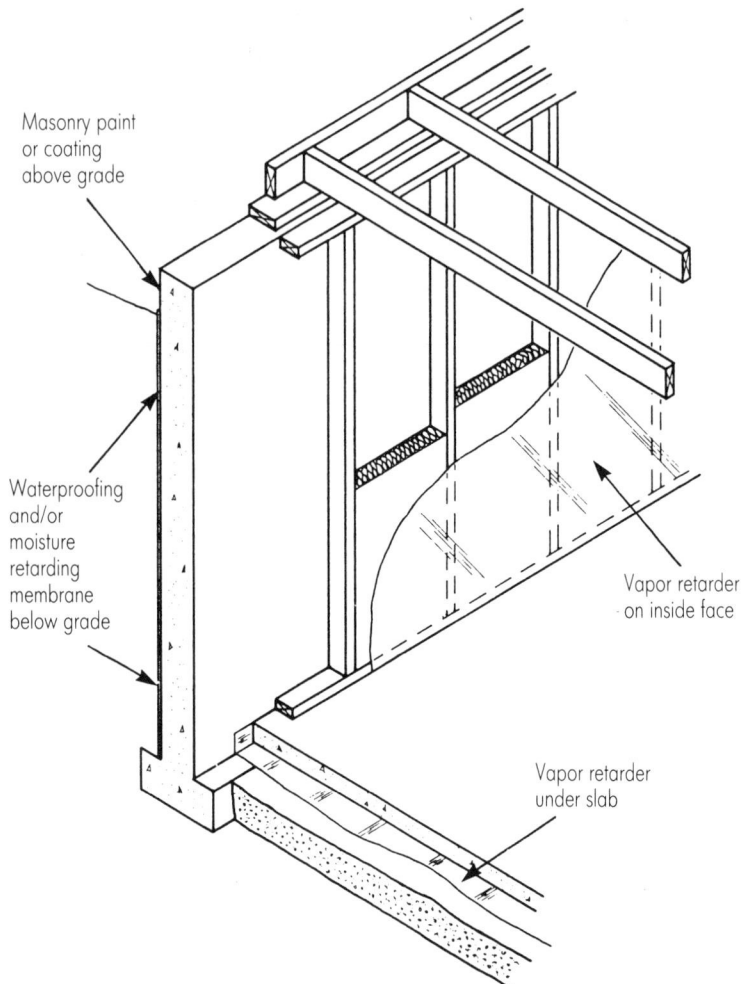

Figure 12: A masonry paint or coating should be applied to the outside of basement walls above grade, and a waterproof coating and/or moisture-retarding membrane below grade. A vapor retarder should be applied to the inside face of insulated basement walls.

- Stop air leakage from the living space into walls and roof/ceiling spaces, particularly at electrical outlets and switches, light fixtures, vent stacks, attic access doors, and any other penetrations in the vapor retarder.
- Ventilate attics and roof spaces with a net vent area equal to at least 1/300 of the ceiling area. When no ceiling vapor retarder is

used, distribute vents equally between high outlets and inlets at eaves. Locate vents to provide cross ventilation.
- Use a moisture-retarding soil cover in crawl spaces. Six-mil polyethylene will provide good puncture resistance. Provide surface drainage away from the building. Install a sump drain or pump in problem areas.
- Ventilate crawl spaces with a net vent area equal to at least 1/1500 of the ground surface area in conjunction with a soil cover. Locate vents to provide cross ventilation.
- Use a moisture-retarding membrane, such as 6-mil polyethylene, under concrete slabs to block moisture from the soil. Use three to four inches of coarse sand or gravel under the membrane to act as a water capillarity break in all but dry, well-drained soils.
- Use a masonry paint or coating on the exterior of basement walls above grade, and a waterproof coating and/or moisture-retarding membrane below grade. Apply a moisture vapor retarder to the warm-in-winter side of basement walls that are insulated on the interior.

Chapter 4
Moisture Control in Warm, Humid Climates

Condensation problems resulting from air conditioning have been observed in the warm, humid region along the South Atlantic and Gulf Coast (Zone 3 on the map in Figure 6). In these areas, air conditioning is operated for long periods of time, and night temperatures remain high. Where warm outdoor air with a high relative humidity gains access to a wall or ceiling, condensation can occur on the back of the interior covering material if it is below the dew point temperature of the air. Condensation can also result on cold floors and other interior surfaces when the indoor relative humidity is excessive.

Indoor Humidity

An indoor relative humidity of 70 percent or more can result in an uncomfortable, clammy feeling—even with a reasonably low temperature setting. Also, condensation forms quite readily on cooler surfaces with a high indoor relative humidity. For example, the psychrometric chart described previously shows that interior air at 75°F with a relative humidity of 80 percent will condense on a surface, such as a concrete slab floor, that is 68°F.

One of the primary functions of conventional air conditioning equipment is dehumidification. As the indoor air comes in contact with the cooling coil, which is below the dew point temperature, excess moisture condenses out and is drained away. The air that is redistributed to the house is both cooler and drier. However, if the air conditioning equipment is oversized, it will cool the air and shut off before it has had a chance to dehumidify the air adequately. Therefore, care should be taken to avoid oversizing air conditioning equipment, especially in view of the lower cooling requirements of today's well-insulated houses.

Evaporative coolers, sometimes called "swamp coolers," cool outdoor air at a relatively low cost by drawing it through a filter that is constantly wetted by a recirculating pump. An effective means of cooling in dry climates, an evaporative cooler contributes desirable moisture to the air in such climates. However, this type of equipment should never be considered in more humid climates.

Vapor Retarders

In the 1960s, surveys indicated that condensation in insulated walls was not generally a problem in houses with indoor temperatures of 75°F or higher. Two major studies conducted in the early 1980s evaluated performance of conditioned buildings in a warm, humid coastal climate. These studies showed that, where an inside vapor retarder was used, a daily cycle of moisture movement occurred, with condensation on the outside of the vapor retarder forming during the day and dissipating at night. Where no inside vapor retarder was used, or where a vapor retarder was placed on both the inside and the outside, condensation did not develop. While no damage to any materials was observed in these studies, the facts pointed to a potential problem.

While no absolute answers exist, prevailing current opinion in the scientific community favors the use of a permeable air barrier rather than a vapor retarder on either side of the wall in warm, humid climates. Accordingly, wall coverings that act as a vapor retarder, such a vinyl wallpapers, should be avoided in such climates.

Masonry Walls

Masonry walls can pose special problems in warm, humid climates. Such problems are particularly pertinent when one considers the great proportion of masonry buildings built in such climates. The musty smell sometimes encountered in masonry buildings in these humid climates indicates the presence of moisture and mildew.

Masonry walls with no insulation pose the greatest problem. However, most masonry homes built today incorporate some form of insulation. The best location for the insulation is on the exterior: for example, plastic foam board attached to the exterior and covered with metal lath and stucco. However, since such methods tend to be more costly than insulating the interior side of the wall, most masonry homes are insulated on the inside using insulation between furring strips or non-loadbearing wood studs. Another method utilizes plastic foam board installed over the interior face of the wall with appropriate adhesive or mechanical fasteners. Gypsum wallboard is then attached to the foam insulation with an adhesive designed for this purpose. Where a vapor-retarding foam board is used, this construction will retard moisture vapor movement in either direction and provide added protection against condensation.

One of the most troublesome sources of moisture in masonry walls is simply rain that penetrates the masonry. It is suspected that many problem cases attributed to condensation actually originate with rain. Silicone treatments, breathable masonry paints, or stucco with special waterproofing additives should be used on the exterior of masonry walls to block the penetration of rain. Special care should also be taken to caulk, seal, and flash properly around windows, doors, and other potential leakage points.

Good Practice Recommendations

- In the hot, humid climate of the South Atlantic and Gulf Coast regions, do not use a vapor retarder on either the inside or outside of walls, and do not use vinyl wallpaper on outer walls.
- Do not oversize air conditioning equipment; oversized equipment will not dehumidify adequately. Use an evaporative cooler only in very dry climates.
- Solid masonry walls should be insulated on either the inside or outside. The exterior surface should be well sealed, and potential leakage points, such as around doors and windows, should be caulked and flashed to prevent penetration of rain water.

Chapter 5
Correcting Existing Problems

Excessive humidity may occasionally be present in new homes. New concrete, for example, contains a great deal of water that is given back to the air over a period of several months. This moisture can prove particularly troublesome when the house is enclosed at the beginning of the heating season. Little opportunity exists for natural ventilation to carry off this water. The only solution is to provide extra ventilation, either by running exhaust fans or periodically opening windows. The new homeowner should be advised of these measures and reassured that any problem with excess moisture will likely resolve itself after the first heating season. However, persistent problems in existing homes may be more difficult to solve.

High Relative Humidity

Many moisture problems in existing homes are a direct result of excessively high indoor humidity. For the greatest degree of accuracy, humidity should be measured with a psychrometer. This device provides dry bulb and wet bulb thermometer readings from which the relative humidity is determined by referring to a table. Other types of humidity gauges are also available.

If the indoor relative humidity exceeds 50 percent during cold weather, action should probably be taken to reduce it. If no means of measuring relative humidity is available, excessive condensation on double-glazed windows in cold weather is an indicator of high humidity. If the condensation has been occurring over a long period, the bottom rails of window sash will be stained with collected water.

The first step in reducing indoor humidity is to look for large sources of moisture. A crawl space with moist soil or standing water, or a damp basement, can substantially increase humidity. The problem may be traced to poor drainage around the house, which can be corrected through proper grading and the channeling of discharge from downspouts away from the house. Other sources of indoor humidity may include numerous house plants, an unvented clothes dryer, green firewood stored indoors, a humidifier, or wet clothes hung to dry in the basement.

If there are no unusual moisture sources, the high humidity may simply be a result of living habits that are difficult to change. In cold climates, the solution may be to provide more ventilation by using existing exhaust fans or adding exhaust fans to the kitchen, bathrooms, or laundry. When a forced air heating system is used, a small duct may be connected to the return side of the furnace duct system to draw in outdoor air, as described previously. In warm climates, it may be necessary to reduce the capacity of the air-conditioning system to obtain adequate dehumidification.

Window Condensation

If excessive window condensation persists on double-glazed windows in cold climates after humidity has been reduced to 40 percent, poorly constructed windows, such as metal-sash units that lack an effective thermal break, may be conducting heat from the interior glass surface. This condition may be corrected by the addition of separate storm windows.

Condensation may occur on the inside surface of storm windows if humid indoor air leaks into the space between the prime window and the storm window. This problem can be corrected by either providing better weatherstripping on the prime window or venting the storm window to the outdoors with small vent holes.

Insulating shutters or doors used over windows on the inside need to be airtight to prevent access of humid indoor air to the cold glass surface.

Attic Moisture

First, determine whether attic moisture is being caused by condensation or windblown rain or snow. If the latter is the culprit, vent adjustments will need to be made to correct the problem. If it is necessary to close a vent off, resulting in inadequate vent area, then an additional vent should be installed elsewhere.

If attic condensation is the problem, make certain that ventilation is adequate and well distributed. If eave vents are used, be sure they are not blocked by insulation. If no eave vents are provided, consider adding them. If no vents are provided high up in the roof, add gable or roof vents near the peak or install a continuous vent at the ridge. Check the ceiling for openings—particularly around attic access doors or vent stacks—that allow moist air to escape into the attic. Any openings should be stuffed with mineral fiber insulation, caulked, taped, or sealed to stop leakage. In some cases, exhaust fans may be vented to the attic; these should be vented to the outside—either through the roof or in some other manner.

If a vapor retarder is not present in a ceiling and is indicated as part of the solution, as in the cold climate of Zone 1, the insulation can be removed and a proper vapor retarder installed before replacing the insulation. As an alternative, vapor resistance can be added by applying a vapor retarder paint to the interior surface of the ceiling. Several major manufacturers offer such paints.

Crawl Space Moisture

Since crawl spaces are generally accessible, most moisture-control measures discussed previously apply equally to existing homes. The most common problems are poor surface drainage away from the house and the lack of a moisture-retarding soil cover. A soil cover should always be used in crawl spaces that have a potential moisture problem. In particularly troublesome cases, a sump may be installed to collect excessive ground water and drain or pump it away. In addition to correcting these conditions, check for adequate cross ventilation of the crawl space, as described previously.

Concrete Surface Condensation

Slab floors, basement walls, and other concrete surfaces are sometimes subject to condensation in late spring when warm, humid air enters the house. The temperature of the concrete surface may be below dew point because the ground below is still cold from winter. Keeping the windows closed and raising the indoor temperature will minimize the problem. When the concrete surface approaches room temperature, this problem will usually disappear.

Condensation can also occur on cool concrete surfaces in warm, humid climates. Where applicable, the best solution is to reduce indoor humidity by downsizing the air conditioning equipment, as described previously.

Exterior Paint Peeling

Since not all exterior paint problems are attributable to condensation, the cause of any peeling paint must first be established. Other causes may be incompatible coats of paint, paint applied under adverse weather conditions, condition of the substrate when painted, or simply a poor quality of paint.

If the peeling is caused by condensation, it will probably be worse on the north side of the house or outside high-moisture areas, such as bathrooms or kitchens, and will not occur on unheated areas such as garages. If condensation is the problem, the most effective treatment is to reduce indoor humidity. Also, stop air leakage into the wall from indoors through electrical outlets, cracks, and joints wherever possible. In cold climates, if there is no vapor retarder in the wall, application of a vapor- retarding paint or vinyl wallpaper, particularly on bathroom and kitchen walls, may also be helpful. Venting the walls is not recommended. As discussed previously, studies have shown that the introduction of cold outside air into the wall cavity can actually contribute to the condensation problem.

Ice Dams

Ice dams are usually visible when they occur. Once they appear, little can be done except to keep snow removed from the roof to eliminate the water source. The main corrective measure is to ensure good distribution of attic ventilation, especially at the eaves. Good ventilation along with adequate ceiling insulation will keep the roof cold and prevent melting. When reroofing, a wide strip of roll roofing may be installed along the eaves before applying the new shingles, as described previously. This will prevent water that is trapped by ice dams from getting through the roof.

References

American Society of Heating, Refrigerating, and Air-Conditioning Engineers. *ASHRAE Handbook of Fundamentals.* New York: ASHRAE, 1985.

Anderson, L.O., and G.E. Sherwood. "Condensation Problems in Your House: Prevention and Solution." *Agricultural Information Bulletin* 373 (USDA, Forest Products Laboratory, Madison, Wis., 1974).

Brown, E.J., W.H. Kapple, and D.H. Percival. *Construction for Attic Ventilation* (Technical Note #9). Champaign, Ill.: Small Homes Council, Building Research Council, University of Illinois, 1974.

Building Thermal Envelope Coordinating Council. *Moisture Control in Buildings* (workshop proceedings, Moisture Control in Buildings Research Coordinating Committee, Washington, D.C., October 1984).

Cutter Information Corporation. *Moisture in Houses: Control Technology for Designers and Builders* (Energy Design Update). Arlington, Mass.: Cutter Information Corp., 1986.

DeMarne, Henry. "Wet Insulation - More Moisture Myths Unmasked." *New England Builder* 4, no. 11 (1986).

Department of Energy. *Control of Condensation in the Walls and Ceilings of Retrofitted Houses.* (Report by Special Ad Hoc Task Group under contract to National Bureau of Standards for Division of Building and Community Systems, 1978).

Drisko, R.W. *Paint Failures—Causes and Remedies* (Techdata Sheet 82-08). Port Hueneme, Calif.: Naval Civil Engineering Laboratory, 1982.

Duff, John E. *Moisture Conditions of a Joist Floor over an Insulated and Sealed Crawlspace* (Forest Service Research Paper SE-206). Asheville, N.C.: Southeast Forest Experiment Station, 1980.

Dutt, G.S. "Condensation in Attics: Are Vapor Barriers Really the Answer?" *Energy and Buildings* 2, no. 4 (study from Center for Energy and Environmental Studies, Princeton University, 1979).

Eyre, D., and D. Jennings. *Air Vapor Barriers.* Ottawa, Ontario: Canadian Oil Substitution Branch, 1981.

H.C. Products Co. *Fundamentals of Residential Attic Ventilation.* Princeville, Ill.: H.C. Products Co., 1974.

H.R. Trechsel Associates. *Problem Definition Study of Requirements for Vapor Barriers in the Building Envelope* (CR 83.D06). Germantown, Md.: H.R. Trechsel Associates, 1982.

Jones, R.A. "Crawlspace Houses" (F.4.4). *Council Notes* 4, no. 2 (Small Homes Council, Building Research Council, University of Illinois at Urbana, 1980).

Marshall, Brian, and Robert Argue. *The Superinsulated Retrofit Book.* Toronto, Ontario: Renewable Energy in Canada Publishers, 1981.

Marshall Macklin Monaghan Limited. *Moisture in NHA Housing.* Ottawa, Canada: Canadian Mortgage and Housing Corporation, 1983.

NAHB Research Foundation. *Basement Water Leakage—Causes, Prevention and Correction.* Washington, D.C.: National Association of Home Builders, 1978.

NAHB Research Foundation. *Insulation Manual—Homes, Apartments.* Washington, D.C.: National Association of Home Builders, 1979.

National Center for Appropriate Technology. *Moisture and Home Energy Conservation.* Butte, Mont.: NCAT, 1983.

National Paint and Coatings Association, Inc. *Mildew.* (Scientific Circular 802) Washington, D.C.: NPCA, 1977.

Rowley, R.B., A.B. Algren, and C.E. Lund. "Condensation of Moisture and Its Relation to Building Construction and Operation." *Bulletin of the University of Minnesota Engineering Extension Station* 18, no. 56 (1941).

Sherwood, G.E. *Condensation Potential in High Thermal Performance Walls— Hot, Humid, Summer Climate* (Research Paper FPL 455). Madison, Wis.: Forest Products Laboratory, 1985.

Sherwood, G.E. *Condensation Potential in High Thermal Performance Walls— Cold, Winter Climate* (Research Paper FPL 433). Madison, Wis.: Forest Products Laboratory, 1983.

Sherwood, G.E. and C.C. Peters. *Moisture Conditions in Walls and Ceilings of an Older Home During Winter* (Research Paper FPL 290). Madison, Wis.: Forest Products Laboratory, 1977.

Sherwood, G.E., and A. TenWolde. "Moisture Movement and Control in Light-Frame Structures." *Forest Products Journal* 32, no. 10 (1982):69-73.

Sherwood, G.E., and A. TenWolde. *Movement and Management of Moisture in Light-Frame Structures* (FPRS Proceedings 7317) and *Wall and Floor Systems: Design and Performance of Light-Frame Structures.* Dubuque, Iowa: Kendall/Hunt Publishing Company, 1983.

Shurcliff, William A. *Air-to-Air Heat Exchangers.* Cambridge, Mass.: Brick House Publishing Co., 1980.

TenWolde, A., and H.T. Mei. "Moisture Movement in Walls in a Warm, Humid Climate." Paper presented at ASHRAE/DOE/BTECC Conference, February, 1986.

TenWolde, A., and J.C. Suleski. "Controlling Moisture in Houses." *Solar Age* (January 1984).

Tsongas, George A., and Sieton, John and Odell, Inc. *Field Study of Moisture Damage in Walls Insulated Without a Vapor Barrier* (Prepared for the Oregon Department of Energy ORNL/SUB-78/97726/I). Oak Ridge, Tenn.: Oak Ridge National Lab, 1980.

Underground Space Center. *Earth Sheltered Housing Design* (2nd ed.) Minneapolis, Minn.: University of Minnesota, 1985.

U.S. Department of Agriculture. *Drainage Around Your Home* (USDA Home and Garden Bulletin No. 210). Washington, D.C.: U.S. Government Printing Office, 1975.

U.S. Department of Agriculture. *Principles for Protecting Wood Buildings From Decay* (Forest Service Research Note FPL-190). Madison, Wis.: U.S. Department of Agriculture, 1973.

U.S. Department of Energy, Office of Assistant Secretary for Conservation and Solar/Office of Building and Community Systems. *Residential Conservation Service (RCS) Auditor Training Manual* (Chapter 7: Moisture Control). Washington, D.C.: U.S. Department of Energy, 1980.

Verrall, A. F. "Condensation in Air-Cooled Buildings." *Forest Journal* 12(12):531-536.

Appendix:
Psychrometrics for Builders and Designers: The Behavior of Moist Air*

With the advent of more sophisticated envelope design for houses, it has become increasingly important for residential designers and builders to understand psychrometrics—the behavior of moist air under various temperature and humidity conditions.

One basic tool is the "psychrometric chart." A full psychrometric chart includes hundreds of lines which describe the physical properties of air over a broad range of temperatures. Most people get dizzy just looking at a complete chart and to master its use is a challenge even for many engineers. Figure 1 is a simplified version of the psychrometric chart. The horizontal axis represents dry-bulb air temperature (dry-bulb temperature is what we're all used to, measured with an ordinary thermometer). The curved lines represent relative humidity.

This simplified psychrometric chart can be used by designers and builders to address several practical moisture-related design issues. We will show how this chart can be used in predicting moisture condensation in several different situations. In addition we will discuss the chart's usefulness in demonstrating how cold winter air can be used in controlling indoor relative humidity.

Predicting Moisture Condensation with the Psychrometric Chart
Some common questions
1. During summer, will condensation occur on an uninsulated basement floor in a warm climate if the basement is ventilated with outdoor air?
2. During winter, will condensation occur on ventilation intake ducts located in a heated basement?
3. Under what conditions will condensation occur on cold water pipes?
4. If a wall is insulated with R-19 fiberglass batts plus R-7 exterior foil-faced foam sheathing, will condensation occur on the inner foil face of the sheathing?

---

*Reproduced with permission from Cutter Information Corporation. *Moisture in Houses: Control Technology for Designers and Builders* (Energy Design Update). Arlington, Mass.: Cutter Information Corp., 1986.

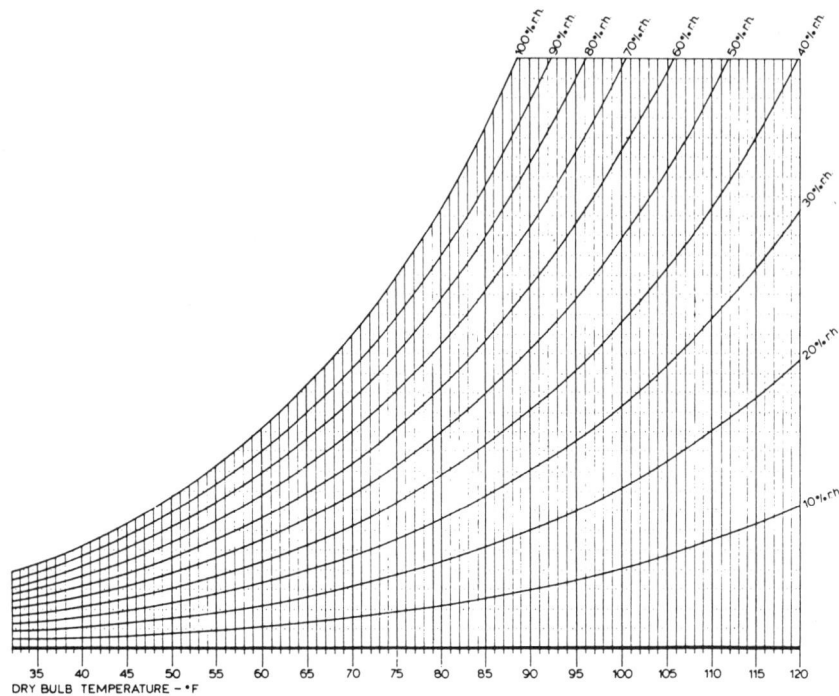

Figure 1: Simplified Psychrometric Chart.

Finding the answers

To predict whether or not moisture condensation will occur on a certain surface, one needs to know three things:

1. The temperature of the air.
2. The relative humidity of the air.
3. The temperature of the surface in question.

Moisture condensation occurs when air is cooled below a certain critical temperature called the "dew-point temperature."

If the temperature of a surface is below the dew-point temperature of the air, condensation will occur.

If we know the temperature and relative humidity, it is easy to determine the dew-point temperature of an air mass by using the psychrometric chart. The following four examples show how to use the chart to determine dew-point temperature and to predict condensation conditions. The first three examples deal with surface condensation on basement floors, ventilation ducts, and cold water pipes. Example 4 is a slightly more complex situation in which we look at the possibility of concealed condensation inside a wall section.

Example 1: Condensation on basement floors.

In warm climates, some designers intentionally avoid sub-slab insulation under basement floors to derive some benefit from ground-coupled cooling. But sometimes those slabs get wet and, although the first suspected culprit is ground-moisture, condensation from interior air may actually be the source. In those cases, it may be advisable to insulate the slab to prevent surface condensation.

As an example, let's look at Houston, Texas, where summer design conditions are about 92°F and 50% relative humidity. If a basement in Houston is ventilated with outdoor air during the summer, is condensation likely to occur on the uninsulated basement floor? (The average ground temperature at 2 to 12 foot depth is about 79°F in summer.)

Solution (Figure 2):

To answer the question, we use the psychrometric chart to determine the dew-point temperature of the air. If the surface temperature of the floor is below the dew-point temperature of the air, condensation will occur.

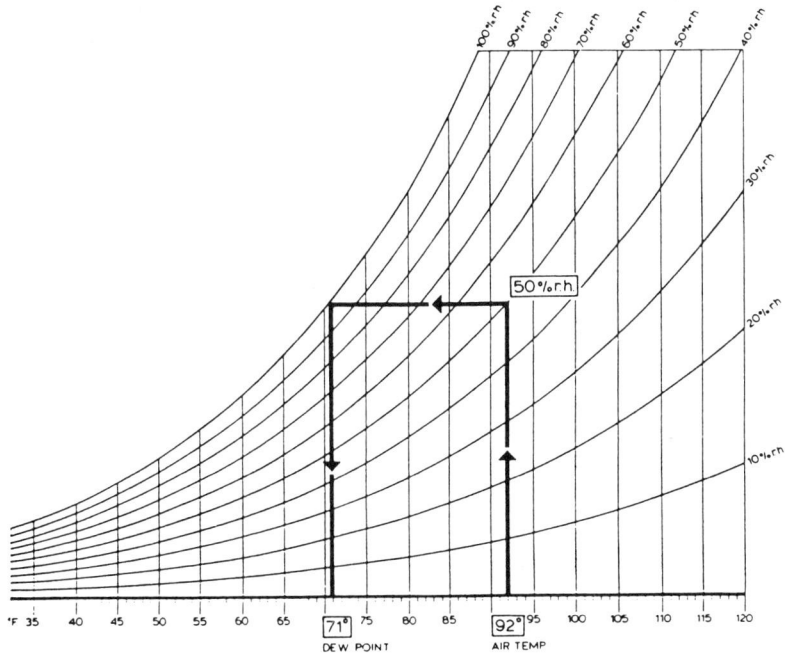

Figure 2: Finding the Dew-Point Temperature of Air at 92°F and 50% rh.

Here's how to use the chart:
1. Find 92°F on the horizontal axis.
2. Follow the line vertically up to the intersection of the curved line marked 50% rh.
3. Proceed horizontally to the left to the intersection with the curved line marked 100% rh.
4. Finally, proceed vertically down to the horizontal axis and read the dew-point temperature—about 71°F.

In this instance, the dew-point temperature of the air is 71°F. Since the average ground temperature in summer, about 79°F, is not below the 71°F dew-point temperature, *condensation should not occur.*

Example 2: Condensation on ventilation ducts.

If fresh air intake ducts for a ventilation system are located in a heated basement, will moisture condense on the outer surface? If so, what should be done?

Solution (Figure 3):

To answer these questions, we first determine the dew-point temperature of the indoor air using the psychrometric chart. Next we estimate typical duct surface temperatures to see if they fall below the air dew-point temperature.

Let's assume the indoor air is at 70°F and 40% rh. The method for determining dew-point temperature is the same as in Example 1.

1. Using the chart, find 70°F on the horizontal axis.
2. Proceed vertically to the curved line marked 40% rh.
3. Proceed horizontally to the left to the intersection with the curved line marked 100%.
4. Finally, proceed downward and read the dew-point temperature—44°F—on the horizontal axis.

Under these indoor conditions, condensation will occur on any surface whose temperature is below 44°F. If winter outdoor air temperatures are often below 44°F for extended periods of time, then condensation on the duct surface will definitely be a problem.

To alleviate the problem, the fresh air intake ducts should be insulated.

Example 3: Condensation on cold water pipes.

Suppose one of your customers discovers water in the plumbing wall behind the bathroom. He suspects a plumbing leak, but there doesn't seem to be enough water for that. He is an elderly man and

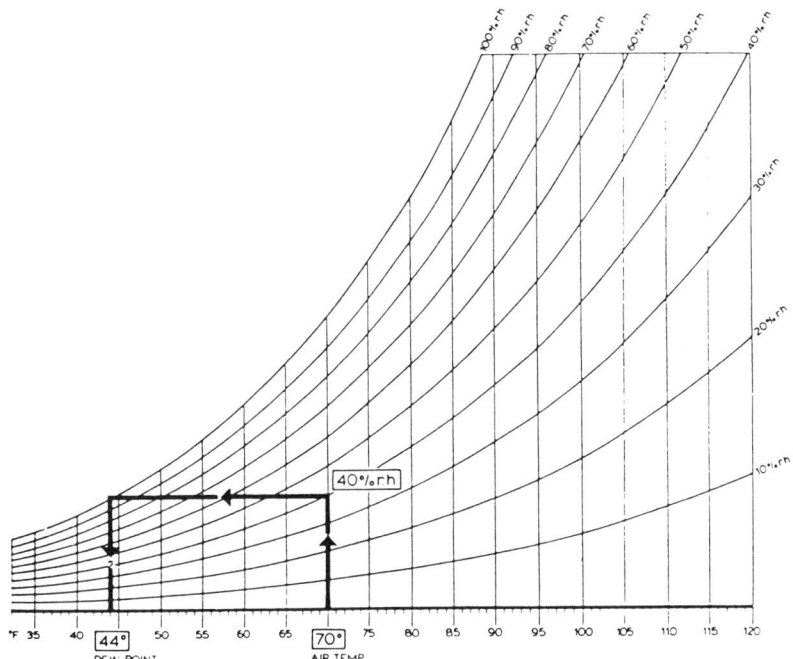

Figure 3: Finding the Dew-Point Temperature of Air at 70°F and 40% rh.

keeps the house at about 78°F. When you visit the house, you measure the relative humidity at 50%. Could the problem be condensation on the cold water pipes? The house used well water from a deep well. The water temperature is about 45°F.

Solution (Figure 4):

Using the psychrometric chart (Figure 4), we see that the dew-point temperature of air at 78°F and 50% rh is about 58°F. Since the cold water temperature is below that (45°F), condensation is probably occurring on the pipes. To remedy the situation, either the relative humidity of the house should be reduced and/or the cold water pipes should be insulated.

Example 4: Concealed condensation in an insulated wall.

Suppose you have designed a wall with 6-inch (R-19) fiberglass batts plus foil-faced exterior foam sheathing (R-7). Since the foil-faced sheathing creates a vapor barrier on the cold side of the fiberglass insulation, there is some concern that condensation might occur on the foil if moist indoor air leaks into the wall cavity. (No condensation will occur if the temperature of the foil is above the dew point of the

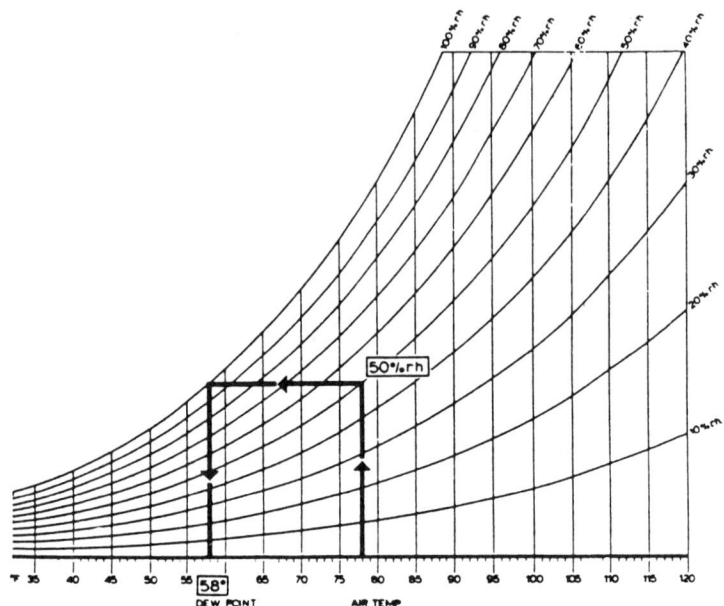

Figure 4: Finding the Dew-Point Temperature of Air at 78°F and 50% rh.

air.) Under average winter conditions, say 35°F outdoor air temperature, will the temperature of the foil facing be above or below the dew-point temperature of the indoor air?

Solution:
This example is slightly more complex because you need to calculate the temperature of the foil. Since there is insulation on both sides (foam on the outside, fiberglass on the inside), the foil temperature will be somewhere between the indoor and outdoor air temperatures.

The following simple procedure can be used to calculate the temperature at any point (P) inside the wall.

1. Calculate the total R-value of the wall. Call this R1.
2. Calculate the R-value of the wall from the inside air to the point (P) that you are interested in. Call this R2.
3. T_i = Indoor temperature.
   T_o = Outdoor temperature.
4. T_p = Temperature at point P.

To find T_p, use the following equation:

$$T_p = T_i - ((T_i - T_o) \times (R2/R1))$$

For this example, we need to find the temperature of the foil when the indoor temperature (Ti) is 70°F and the outdoor temperature (To) is 35°F. The R-values are taken from Figure 5.

1. R1 = 28.72
2. R2 = 20.13
3. Ti = 70°F
   To = 35°F
4. Tp = 70 − ((70 − 35) x (20.13/28.72)) = 45°F

Thus the temperature of the foil surface will be 45°F when the outdoor air is 35°F and the indoor air is 70°F.

In Example 2, we found that the dew-point temperature of air at 70°F and 40% rh is about 44°F (Figure 3)—slightly below the 45°F foil temperature. Thus, no condensation should occur under these temperature conditions. It is, however, a borderline case; if the outdoor air temperature were to drop, condensation might occur.

You can perform this calculation for any wall design and temperature regime. Keep in mind that it cannot exactly predict when condensation will occur because of complicating factors such as parallel heat flow through studs, insulation imperfections, air leaks, etc. Also, keep in mind that moisture condensation in walls with exterior sheathing is quite complex and not fully understood. In many cases, no evidence of condensation is found even though calculations show that it should occur. But the calculations are good insurance. If they show that condensation will not occur under average winter conditions, then one can confidently assume that no moisture problems from condensation will occur.

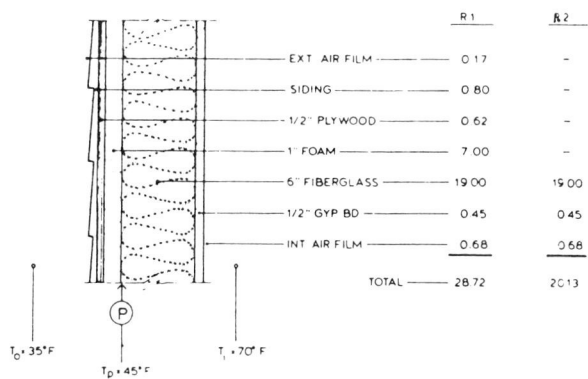

Figure 5: Finding the Temperature at a Point P in a Wall.

47

Understanding "Dry Winter Air"

Another important application of this chart is in demonstrating the effectiveness of ventilation techniques. For instance, the psychrometric chart explains why outdoor air can be used to lower the humidity in a house even though the outdoor air may have a considerably higher relative humidity than the indoor air.

The explanation is actually quite simple. Relative humidity is a measure of "percent saturation" of water vapor in air. Cold air can hold less water vapor than warm air. For example, air at 35°F can hold a maximum of 0.0043 pounds of moisture per pound of dry air at saturation. If outdoor air at 35°F has, say, 70% of that amount of moisture (0.0030 pounds per pound dry air), we say it is 70% saturated and has a relative humidity of 70%. Now suppose we bring outdoor air at 35°F and 70% rh into a house and heat it to 70°F. Let's assume *no moisture is added or removed from the air.* At 70°F, air can hold 3.4 times as much moisture as air at 35°F (0.0158 lb. per lb. dry air). Thus, even though this air was nearly saturated when it was outside (70% rh), it is nowhere near saturated when it is brought indoors and heated. In fact, the relative humidity is now only 19% (see Figure 6).

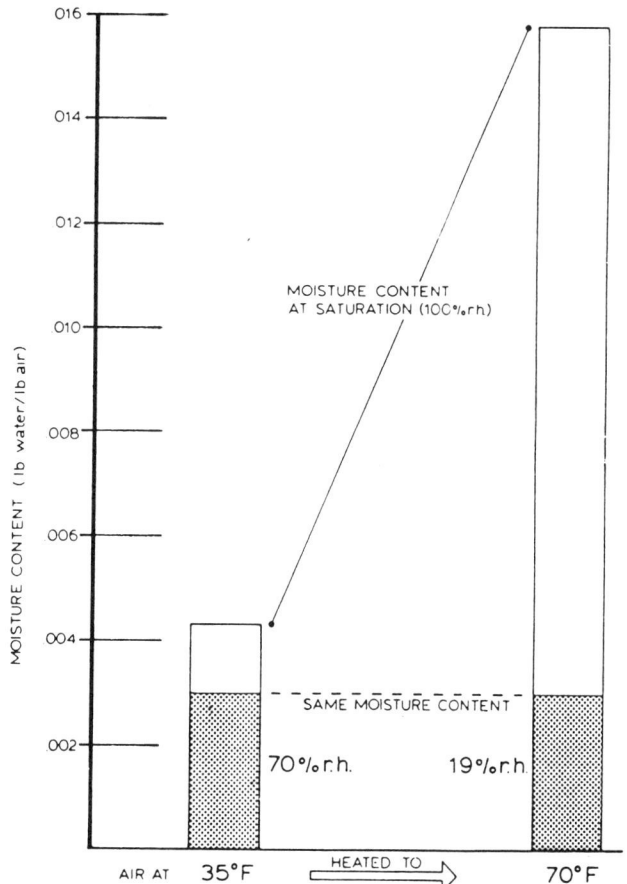

Figure 6: Graph Showing the Change in Relative Humidity of Air at 35°F and 70% rh When Heated to 70°F With No Moisture Added or Removed.

The change in relative humidity when dry winter air is brought into a house is easy to determine using the psychrometric chart. Here's a quick example:

Example 5

If outdoor air has a temperature of 40°F and a relative humidity of 60%, what will be its relative humidity if it is brought into a house and heated to 75°F?

Solution (Figure 7):

1. Find 40°F on the horizontal axis.
2. Proceed vertically to the intersection of the curved line marked 60% rh.
3. Proceed horizontally to the right to the intersection with the vertical line marked 75°F.
4. The relative humidity of the air is read from the curved lines. In this case, it is between 10% and 20%—about 18%.

In this situation, if no moisture were added to the air from indoor sources, the indoor relative humidity would be 18%. Of course, if the house is occupied, quite a bit of moisture is given off from occupant

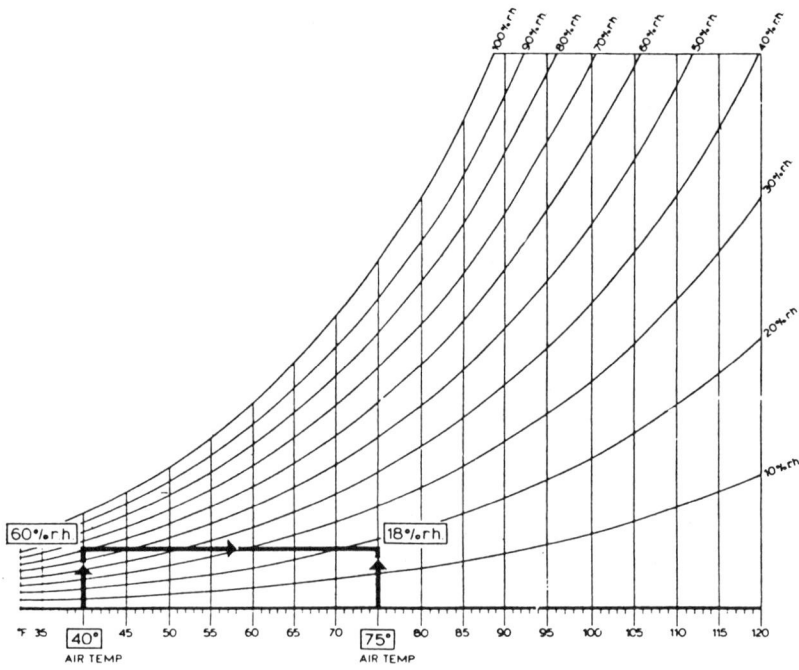

Figure 7: Finding the Relative Humidity of Air at 40°F and 60% rh When Heated to 75°F.

activity and the actual indoor relative humidity will be somewhat higher, depending upon the rate of indoor moisture generation and outdoor air leakage and ventilation.

For more information on the use of the psychrometric chart, see the *ASHRAE Handbook of Fundamentals*, published by ASHRAE, 1791 Tullie Circle N.E., Atlanta, GA 30329.